RANIERI REVERSE RECALL

A METHOD OF MEMORIZATION APPLIED TO LIFE

BY

LUKE AMADEUS RANIERI

ISBN: 9781520498164

AQUELLIA

PUBLISHING
Kintnersville, PA
www.LukeRanieri.com

For my students.

CONTENTS

INTRODUCTION

I N THIS BRIEF TEXT I WOULD LIKE TO TELL YOU OF A WAY to learn anything by heart. It has helped me enormously through the years and I have enjoyed sharing it with classmates and students. While I have on rare occasions stumbled across others who have heard of something like my method, I have never seen anyone adopt it as variously as I have woven it into my own life. Therefore it seemed like a good idea to write the ideas down for a wider audience. This book will quickly present the technique in abstract, and from there I will recount my discovery and its application over the past dozen or so years. Most useful to the reader will be the practice sections which allow one to apply immediately the technique of Ranieri Reverse Recall.

While the key to wisdom is questioning beliefs and assumptions, the key to knowledge is rote recall. The latter 20th and the 21st centuries have seen the diminishment of rote memorization as a supported pedagogical method in most schools with which I have been familiar (indeed, I cannot

1

remember any grade level or class I took where rote memorization was emphasized or even suggested). It has been something I have had to teach myself. As an educator I firmly believe that any student with a mind and a desire to learn can indeed learn a thing, no matter what it is and no matter the person's background or self-perceived limitations, and therefore *all* possible learning techniques should be made available to the student. Visual learners, kinesthetic learners, auditory learners, tactile learners, whatever they might be, can benefit from acquiring knowledge more efficiently. Wisdom is necessary to comprehend the gravity of events, but facts and data are necessary to inform that wisdom. As John Adams said in 1770, "Facts are stubborn things; and whatever may be our wishes, our inclinations, or the dictates of our passion, they cannot alter the state of facts and evidence."

THE TECHNIQUE

Whatever it is you have to recite by heart, learn the last part first and then add backwards.

If this explanation seems glib, forgive me. Read on to find out how I happened upon this idea, the wondrous results in my life of its faithful employment, and how you too can enrich your experiences and knowledge.

CHAPTER 1

OF CRETANS & ODES TO GRECIAN WORDS

I WAS STUDYING ABROAD IN FLORENCE AT THE CENTER OF Foreign Students, a full immersion program for those already conversant in the Italian language. I am second-generation Italian-American and the proud son of a brilliant artist who has taught me all about the culture, the architecture, the artwork of the homeland of his parents. So living in that exquisite country in the spring semester of my sophomore year of college was my dream come true. It was January 2005 and the cool air was fresh and fragrant with the scent of cypresses that ringed the schoolhouse, a converted villa in the countryside far outside the downtown bustle of the

Tuscan capital. My affection for Italy was growing day by day at this excellent institution, and my curiosity was further piqued by the chance to interact with people from other nations.

   During a break between classes, I sat at a small wrought iron table with ceramic mosaic top, sitting across from two incredibly beautiful young ladies about my age with whom I was enjoying coffee. They were Cretans — though decent and trustworthy, I assure you — and were helping me to learn a few Greek phrases. In my notebook I had written Πώς ονομάζεστε — *Pós onomázeste*, "What's your name," which in retrospect seems like it should have been easy to pronounce. Perhaps it was due to the Greek alphabet with which I was at that time only shallowly familiar, or to the penetrating dark eyes and radiant smile of the girl patiently reciting the line in that mellifluous tongue. Whatever the cause, I found myself incapable of repeating it accurately. In that moment of frustration I was touched by the very mother of the muses, and it occurred to me what to do. My pen followed the syllables from the end of the word and I spoke them aloud in this order:

te

zes - te

zeste

má - zeste

mázeste

no - mázeste

nomázeste

o - nomázeste

onomázeste

pós onomázeste

My words were smooth and my accent was true! Just like that I had cracked the code securing even the toughest of long words. The Ranieri Reverse Recall method was born.

At the time I had no idea of the extensive applications possible with this technique. But I was aware generally of *why* it worked. When trying to say a long and unfamiliar word, one attempts to sound out one syllable at a time from start to finish. Though often taught to do so in school, native English speakers are especially bad at this because English spelling is historical and not particularly phonetic. When you read these words at a normal pace, you will tend to ignore the vowels and the middle parts of the word, and unconsciously allow the consonants and the initial and final letters to tell you what it is. Thus a sequential syllabic dissection comes unnaturally to us.

Moreover, while slogging through the first syllable and groping for the second, the unfamiliar terrain of the word abandons the reader in a deep swamp of muddy unfamiliarity, and each hard-earned step forward means a footprint behind submerged again under the mire. So instead, don't be a slave to the fourth dimension: leap off the surface, and carve out a path at the end and work backwards.

By concentrating on the final sequence of sounds first, they become ingrained more readily into short-term memory. But going backwards alone is not the solution — starting towards the end and running the clock *forwards* is the real key. Thus every previous syllable added to the line means retreading the second-to-last and final syllables again and again. You already remember where you are going, and so it becomes automatic.

Take the Greek example above. Before I was done, I had said the final syllable *te* a total of ten times, the second-to-last syllable *zes* eight times, and so forth, giving the initial word *pós* only a single utterance. But then as I spoke each following syllable of the whole phrase — *pós o-no* — I would tread into ever more familiar territory — *má-zes-te* — and was pulled forward through the muck of my former confusion to the crystal-clear end.

PRACTICE SECTION

Can you think of a word or phrase, whether in English or from a foreign language, that you have trouble pronouncing? Jot it down, and read on to see how to apply the method exactly.

CHAPTER 2

DIFFICULT NAMES

A FAVORITE COMEDY OF MINE IS THE 1999 FILM
Office Space, and one of the characters has the last
name Nagheenanajar. This mid-level employee's plight is to
experience daily his coworkers' and bosses' obtuse inability to
wrap their mouths around his name. Samir Nagheenanajar
passively accepts this minor humiliation, as many do with
difficult names, but he cannot escape the emasculation he
feels. For a man's name is very important to him, as John
Proctor cried aloud in *The Crucible* to explain why he refused
to turn over his false confession of witchcraft and preferred to
hang: "Because it is my name! Because I cannot have another
in my life."

So to ease Samir Nagheenanajar in spirit, let us apply Ranieri Reverse Recall to the challenge. We will assume that the 'gh' is silent and the stressed syllable is the 'ee' (italicized below), matching the actor's pronunciation. Say each syllable out loud in the order presented (pause at the hyphens, and read fluently elsewhere):

jar

na - jar

najar

na - najar

nanajar

ee
(the stressed syllable)

nanajar

ee - nanajar

*ee*nanajar

Nagh

(the 'gh' is silent)

*ee*nanajar

Nagh - *ee*nanajar

Nagh*ee*nanajar

If you followed the above path exactly, you probably found it fairly easy to get through the whole name without too much trouble. You may even have needed fewer steps than presented here, but I have chosen to show my work in the backwards arithmetic of the syllables to illustrate the example fully. Just like Samir said in the movie, "It's not that hard."

While on the topic of long foreign-sounding names that start with 'n', let us review another comic icon, *The Simpsons* character Apu Nahasapeemapetilon, and apply the method:

lon

ti - lon

tilon

pe

(this is the stressed syllable)

pe - tilon

*pe*tilon

ma - *pe*tilon

ma*pe*tilon

pee - ma*pe*tilon

peema*pe*tilon

sa - peema*pe*tilon

sapeema*pe*tilon

ha - sapeema*pe*tilon

hasapeema*pe*tilon

Na - hasapeema*pe*tilon

Nahasapeema*pe*tilon

You who read this know already that I do not have an easily pronounceable last name. My time in Florence was joyous on many levels, but it was exemplary to hear "Ranieri" announced correctly and beautifully by my Italic kin. In the Anglosphere, however, and in America in particular where we are blessed by a thousand mixing peoples but cursed by a thousand unpronounceable surnames, most English speakers give up quickly on approximating the thing. I would never expect an American to trill the 'r's or use any set of sounds outside of our English phonotactic limitations, and in fact as a matter of preference I rather insist all of us with names of non-Anglo-Saxon origin conform them to the set of possible English language sounds.

That said, the Anglicized version of "Ranieri" must be as follows. 'Ran-' is the same as the past tense verb "ran"; '-ier-' rhymes with "air" but has a 'y'-sound in front of it, so we could write it as *'yair'* to give us a sense of it; and finally '-i' sounds like the 'i' in "machine." At the risk of being nakedly self-serving, I will walk you through it:

i

ier

(the stressed syllable)

ier - i

*ier*i

Ran - *ier*i

Ran*ier*i

Now you can use Ranieri Reverse Recall, and pronounce it too!

The doubling repetitions help our short-term memory to grab hold of the syllables farthest down on the word. While these doublings may be omitted, it is best not to rush. Aim for accuracy the the first time, and then develop speed. Speedily learning something the wrong way will get you nowhere fast.

So if your last name is Smith or Jones or May, have pity on your polysyllabic acquaintances, and show them the respect you take for granted with your facile moniker. Do not settle for their obliging response, "That's good enough; don't worry about it." Press them to enunciate their names as they themselves say them, write down the whole thing, and use Ranieri Reverse Recall. They will certainly appreciate the effort.

PRACTICE SECTION

1. Take the word or expression you wrote down from the practice section of Chapter 1, and apply Ranieri Reverse Recall.

2. Use the technique for these challenging names of American Indian origin: Paupukkeewis, Chektowaga, Winaugusconey, Wozhupiwi.

3. Full names of some NHL players: Reijo Ruotsalainen, Sergei Krivokrasov, Vladimir Tsyplakov, Gene Achtymichuk, Igor Vyazmikin, Mathias Tjarnqvist, Jaroslav Svejkovsky, Petteir Nokelainen, Maxim Afinogenov, Maxim Balmochnykh, Bengt-Ake Gustafsson, Ilkka Heikkinen, Kyosti Karjalainen, Ivan Novoseltsev, Branko Radivojevic, Pekka Rautakallio.

4. Some intimidating German words: Eichhörnchen (squirrel), Quietscheentchen (rubby ducky), Schlittschuhaufen (ice skating), fünfhundertfünfundfünfzig (five hundred fifty-five), Streichholzschächtelchen (little match box), Obergruppenführer (a Nazi SS rank equivalent to lieutenant colonel, as depicted in the distopic Amazon series *The Man in the High Castle*), Nordrheinwestfalen (North-Rhine Westphalia).

5. Now try these full names of individuals from India: Marutthur Gopalamenon Pamachandaran, Singanlluru Puttaswamayya Mutthuraju, Villupuram Chinnaih Pillai Ganesan, Pilavullakandi Thekkaparambil Usha, Avul Pakir Jainilabdeen Abdul Kalam Mankkayar, Mangalampalli Balamurali Krishna, Palaghat Kolungode Vishwnatha Narayanaswamye.

CHAPTER 3

NUMBERS & PASSWORDS

T he benefits of Ranieri Reverse Recall are most apparent
when learning something that must be remembered in a
specific sequence. One of the hardest sequences for most
people is a string of numbers.

PHONE NUMBERS

Modern devices reduce the need to memorize
telephone numbers as once was common, but let us give it a
shot anyway. We will start with the phone number 212-555-
2368, which will ring the Ghostbusters. The key here will be

to memorize each of the below lines before proceeding to the next one.

8

68

368

2368

5-2368

55-2368

555-2368

2-555-2368

12-555-2368

212-555-2368

CREDIT CARD NUMBERS

Could we try it with a credit card number? Absolutely.
Here I have imagined a number that should be too long to be a
real one: 3691 8576 2381 5067 5482. One trick I picked up in
Italy when dealing with long numbers is to pronounce a two-
digit number with the tens and ones place, that is to
pronounce "3691" *not* as **a**) "three-six-nine-one" but as **b**)
"thirty-six ninety-one." The reason this is helpful is that one
can hold in one's head two numbers (as with **b**) from one to
ninety-nine fairly easily, while trying to hold four verbalized
numbers (as with **a**) is considerably harder. That means that
the above twenty-digit figure is actually a string of just ten
numbers. I have used a dot to separate two-digit pairs meant
to be pronounced as in **b** above. I recommend repeating each
line to yourself as many times as necessary to memorize that
line and looking away from the page while doing so. Commit
to memory each line before adding more to it; building on
shaky ground is never advisable.

82

54.82

67 54.82

50.67 54.82

81 50.67 54.82

23.81 50.67 54.82

76 23.81 50.67 54.82

85.76 23.81 50.67 54.82

91 85.76 23.81 50.67 54.82

36.91 85.76 23.81 50.67 54.82

If you took care to memorize each line before moving on, you probably got this one into your short-term memory. Assuming you probably do not want to keep this one on mental file, worry not, for without exercises to ingrain the above number into your long-term memory, the above sequence will fade away in a matter of minutes. How to make sure such sequences remain in your long-term memory is the subject of the final chapter of this book.

PASSWORDS

You may have realized that Ranieri Reverse Recall can be employed with passwords as well. Passwords are necessarily becoming longer and more complicated these days. As passwords are typed, there is a strong factor of muscle memory which we can take advantage of in appealing to our tactile learning ability. Here is a perfectly bizarre password: **6wKXkzJWFKhzfaes**. For practicing this, I recommend having access to a keyboard or other device where typing is possible. In each of the steps below, it is imperative that you memorize the line before moving on (you know you have successfully memorized the line if you can type it from short-term memory without looking at the original text). Memorize by repeating the typing of each line before proceeding to the next. This may take several repetitions, especially as the string gets longer:

s

es

aes

faes

zfaes

hzfaes

Khzfaes

FKhzfaes

FKhzfaes

WFKhzfaes

JWFKhzfaes

zJWFKhzfaes

kzJWFKhzfaes

XkzJWFKhzfaes

KXkzJWFKhzfaes

wKJkzJWFKhzfaes

6wKXkzJWFKhzfaes

Now you don't have to shy away from strong passwords, even those completely devoid of words and sounds. The only password that should be **GUEST** is the one for the ISIS Mainframe, and the only passcode that should be **12345** ought only to belong to President Skroob.

JAPANESE NUMBERS

As a teacher of that wholly foreign yet magnificent tongue of the Land of the Rising Sun, I can attest that mastering the Japanese number and counting system can confound even the Japanese themselves. Though most of those challenges lie outside the scope of this book, the initial difficulty presents itself in learning the basic numbers from one to ten. While the basic numbers of other languages like Spanish or French are quite a bit more familiar to us English speakers, the Japanese digits are exotic indeed, and so make for an excellent example to train ourselves. Transliterated into our alphabet, they are:

1	2	3	4	5	6	7	8	9	10
ichi	ni	san	yon	go	roku	nana	hachi	kyuu	juu

The first step is to say the English number followed by the Japanese number in order from one to ten. Then go to the end, and work backwards while moving forwards; as before, you must memorize each line before moving on. Be sure to picture the Arabic numeral while you say aloud the words:

juu

kyuu, juu

hachi, kyuu, juu

nana, hachi, kyuu, juu

roku, nana, hachi, kyuu, juu

go, roku, nana, hachi, kyuu, juu

yon, go, roku, nana, hachi, kyuu, juu

san, yon, go, roku, nana, hachi, kyuu, juu

ni, san, yon, go, roku, nana, hachi, kyuu, juu

ichi, ni, san, yon, go, roku, nana, hachi, kyuu, juu

Utilizing this technique, I have seen students cut their recall time in half. The homework I give them is to count things with these numbers whenever you see their Arabic numerals or on any other occasion, in order to implant the above into long-term memory. Do this homework assignment along with Ranieri Reverse Recall to learn any set of numerals in record time.

PRACTICE SECTION

1. Do you know by heart the phone number of a close family member or dear friend? If not, write it down and apply Ranieri Reverse Recall.

2. Memorize one of your bank card numbers.

3. Learn π (pi) up to fourteen decimal places: 3.14159265358979. My trick is to do this in two-digit terms, reciting "three point fourteen, fifteen, ninety-two, sixty-five, thirty-five, eighty-nine, seventy-nine."

4. Come up with a truly secure password to replace one of your weakest. Memorize it.

5. Learn at least one of the following sets of numbers from 1 to 10:

Italian	French	Spanish	Latin	German	Russian
uno	un	uno	unus	eins	odin
due	deux	dos	duo	zwei	dva
tre	trois	tre	tres	drei	tri
quattro	quatre	cuatro	quattuor	vier	chitiri
cinque	cinq	cinco	quinque	fünf	pyat'
sei	six	seis	sex	sechs	shest'
sette	sept	siete	septem	sieben	syem'
otto	huit	ocho	octo	acht	vosim'
nove	neuf	nueve	novem	neun	dyevit'
dieci	dix	diez	decem	zehn	dyesit'

CHAPTER 4

ENTERING LATINITY

T HE YEAR 2005 WAS SEMINAL TO MY LIFE IN MANY RESPECTS. I happened upon Ranieri Reverse Recall, learned Italian fluently, and even taught myself Latin. I realize I may appear ostentatious by listing these accomplishments so casually. Such activities as studying foreign languages for fun are genuinely interesting to me. And as I mention above, I have my artist-father to thank for exciting my childhood fascination with Renaissance and Classical culture. (Also, I confess, there was a young teacher in my high school who was very pretty, and due to her parents' missionary work in Europe she was fluent in several languages from a young age. I admired her greatly, and had quite a crush on her — so that might have had something to do with it too.) But in any case, I must refute any claim that I have a special talent for foreign languages. I assure you I do not. The only thing I had was the *desire* to pursue Italian and Latin, among others, due to the reasons given above. As I tell all my students, if you can cultivate the desire to learn a thing, and can be given the proper tools to accomplish the task, you *will* learn it. And as for tools, my Swiss Army knife has always been Ranieri Reverse Recall.

So it came to pass that I eagerly wanted to learn Latin, and even to speak it fluently. After being deeply disappointed in traditional textbooks, I took to the internet and found an engrossing webpage by a Rutgers University professor named William C. Dowling, who wrote at length about his Dowling Method to fluency in Latin. In his booklet he relates that Latin is a highly inflected language, meaning that nouns and verbs have many different forms that may be classified into groups with recurring patterns. The key to mastering Latin is to commit these patterns to memory.

Here is one of those paradigms for what is known as the First Declension:

	singular	**plural**
Nominative Case	puella *"the girl" as the subject*	puellae *"the girls" as the subject*
Genitive Case	puellae *"of the girl"*	puellārum *"of the girls"*
Dative Case	puellae *"to the girl"*	puellīs *"to the girls"*
Accusative Case	puellam *"the girl" as the direct object*	puellās *"the girls" as the direct object*
Ablative Case	puellā *"by the girl"*	puellīs *"by the girls"*

There are several dozen paradigms like this. In his brief treatise, Professor Dowling gives the following instructions: (1) understand the basic concepts of the noun and verb systems, which he explains in the booklet, (2) commit all the paradigms to memory by rewriting them 200 times without error, and (3) read the best language-learning textbook of all time, *Lingua Latina* by Hans Ørberg. In doing so, one can achieve fluency in reading Latin in two years, Dowling says. I thought I could speed that process up a bit.

Since remembering a paradigm in order is helpful, I applied Ranieri Reverse Recall to get the thing into short-term memory, and then, once I was capable of reciting it without looking at the original, I began the process of rewriting it 200 times from short-term memory, per Professor Dowling's recommendation. It worked! In a week I had them all down pat, and then proceeded to consume the book *Lingua Latina*. *Lingua Latina* is a reader, telling a story with pleasing characters that ingeniously teaches all aspects of Latin grammar and vocabulary needed for fluency by means of the Latin language alone.

I decided to approach the task of reading *Lingua Latina* uniquely. Because the syntax of Latin is quite unlike English or Italian, I set myself upon transcribing the entire 300-page book of high quality Latin sentences cover to cover. Ambitious? Certainly. But it seemed like it could be an effective means of achieving rapid fluency. Using my recall technique I would memorize a whole sentence or two, then type it, transcribing a whole chapter in this way, line by line. By the end I was fluent in reading and also writing Latin. Although the project of rewriting the book required more man-hours up front, rather than the two years suggested by Professor Dowling, I had learned Latin in only three months.

My life was changed forever. More than a thousand years of Latin literature was suddenly available to me in the original, and that was just the beginning. I would never again be deterred by any task I set myself upon.

PRACTICE SECTION

As a fluent speaker of English, it is hardly necessary to memorize grammatical paradigms; you know the right forms through exposure. But some irregular verbs present problems, especially for foreigners learning our language who have to memorize a table of irregular English verbs like in the chart below (which is not even close to comprehensive). English is a rather simple language grammatically, but this is definitely its hardest aspect. Have pity on them!

Some native English speakers do have trouble, however. A particular pet peeve of mine is to hear "ran" being used as the past participle. For example, hearing something like "that machine was <u>ran</u> five times last week" makes me angry and sad at the same time. The past participle is "<u>*run*</u>." The mixup is understandable; "run" does not sound like it is past tense since it sounds the same as the form used in the present tense.

Another extremely prevalent confusion is with the verbs "lay, laid, laid" and "lie, lay, lain." The verb "to lay" is transitive meaning it may take a direct object; for example, "I am going to <u>lay</u> the plate on the table;" "I <u>laid</u> the plate on the table next to the cup;" "The plate was <u>laid</u> on the table by me." The verb "to lie" is intransitive, and may not be followed by a direct object: "I want to <u>lie</u> down and go to sleep;" "Last night

I lay down in bed at 11:30 P.M.;" "I've lain in bed for nine hours already so I think it's time to get up." I appreciate the difficulty of keeping these straight, and I used to make these kinds of mistakes too; "lay" could be either the simple past of "to lie" or the present tense of "to lay." The words do in fact have a common etymology, which is why they are so similar.

The intransitive verb for stretching out horizontally "lie, lay, lain" is also confused with the mendacious verb "lie, lied, lied." You may have heard a person say, "I lied in bed way past my alarm and was late for work." Well, if that acquaintance was being dishonest with himself and falsely believed the alarm to be incorrect, then I suppose he "lied" in bed indeed — but he also *lay* there quite a while, too.

So the next time a dog with an empty mouth is told to "lay down" and does not move into the prone, he is a very good boy! He knew his grammar: he would need to have a stick or a tennis ball in his mouth to *lay* anything down. He will be very happy to *lie* down for you, however. And no matter how many times a dog has lain down for you or laid a stick at your feet, I can assure you he has never lied to you and is incapable of doing so.

If these or any other verbs have stirred a bit of confusion in you, then this is a good thing! and a golden opportunity. Write down the paradigms of those difficult conjugations, and memorize them like a foreigner might in learning English. Then you have a table in your mind which you can always refer to. Use Ranieri Reverse Recall to internalize any or several of the following verb conjugations. If English is your second language, make sure you know *all* of them by heart.

Present	Simple Past	Past Participle	Present	Simple Past	Past Participle
be	was/were	been	let	let	let
begin	began	begun	lie	lay	lain
break	broke	broken	lose	lost	lost
bring	brought	brought	make	made	made
buy	bought	bought	mean	meant	meant
build	built	built	meet	met	met
choose	chose	chosen	pay	paid	paid
come	came	come	prove	proved	proven, proved
cost	cost	cost	put	put	put
cut	cut	cut	run	ran	run
do	did	done	say	said	said
draw	drew	drawn	see	saw	seen
drive	drove	driven	sell	sold	sold
eat	ate	eaten	send	sent	sent
feel	felt	felt	set	set	set
find	found	found	sit	sat	sat
get	got	got, gotten	speak	spoke	spoken

give	gave	given	spend	spent	spent
go	went	gone	stand	stood	stood
have	had	had	take	took	taken
hear	heard	heard	teach	taught	taught
hold	held	held	tell	told	told
keep	kept	kept	think	thought	thought
know	knew	known	understand	understood	understood
lay	laid	laid	wear	wore	worn
leave	left	left	win	won	won
lead	led	led	write	wrote	written

CHAPTER 5

OF POETS & PATRONS

I F YOU NEED TO LEARN LINES FOR A PLAY, THERE CAN BE
few better ways to start than my recall technique. A great
many classic plays are organized into metric poetry, whose
rhythm and rhymes are very helpful to stimulating one's
recall. And with respect to verses, a particular gift you can
give yourself is to learn by heart a favorite poem that has held
meaning for you.

While I was in Florence I was exposed to some
wonderful Italian poetry, and that year having recently
discovered Ranieri Reverse Recall I decided to experiment
with it. The subject of that early test was the beginning of the
poem *Trionfo di Bacco e Arianna* written by Lorenzo de' Medici
in the 15th century:

Quant'è bella giovinezza
che si fugge tuttavia!
Chi vuol esser lieto, sia:
di doman non c'è certezza.

Here is my somewhat free translation:

How charmed and sweet our days of youth
which flee so quickly day by day!
Be merry one and all, I say:
tomorrow there's no certain truth.

Rather than memorize the Italian version, let us apply the method to the English version. We start with the final line first.

tomorrow there's no certain truth.

Divide the line into whatever chunks desired. The goal is to build backwards without going too fast for your short-term memory to keep up. I will do so with a somewhat conservative approach:

truth.

certain truth.

no certain truth.

there's no certain truth.

tomorrow there's no certain truth.

As before, ensure you have memorized each of these lines before proceeding. Now, when adding backwards from the previous line, we include everything forward that has already been learned:

I say:
tomorrow there's no certain truth.

one and all, I say:
tomorrow there's no certain truth.

Be merry one and all, I say:
tomorrow there's no certain truth.

The iambic meter makes it especially easy to remember the lines (which is a reason for many of Shakespeare's verses being written in it). We continue:

> day by day!
> Be merry one and all, I say:
> tomorrow there's no certain truth.

> so quickly day by day!
> Be merry one and all, I say:
> tomorrow there's no certain truth.

> which flee so quickly day by day!
> Be merry one and all, I say:
> tomorrow there's no certain truth.

> youth
> which flee so quickly day by day!
> Be merry one and all, I say:
> tomorrow there's no certain truth.

> days of youth
> which flee so quickly day by day!
> Be merry one and all, I say:
> tomorrow there's no certain truth.

our days of youth
which flee so quickly day by day!
Be merry one and all, I say:
tomorrow there's no certain truth.

How charmed and sweet our days of youth
which flee so quickly day by day!
Be merry one and all, I say:
tomorrow there's no certain truth.

Having memorized these and other poems, I was able to fit in nicely with other Italians who know these verses by heart as well. But while they had a lifetime to be indoctrinated with them, my recall technique allowed me to catch up rapidly.

In late 2005, just weeks before the end of my study abroad program, I had set out on a great journey across Italy from Florence through Rome and on to the mountainous region of Abruzzo to find the rural hometowns of my grandparents. They had passed away before my birth but their influence on my character was profoundly felt by way of my father. My pilgrimage to Abruzzo was a means for me to connect with them and my heritage. Trains were delayed by December snow, and upon my arrival I was denied lodging in the ski resort of Roccaraso, the birthplace of my grandmother Ada d'Alessandro, since the village was filled with tourists.

Despondent that my trek there had been in vain, I returned to the station just barely in time to catch the last train back to the regional hub of Sulmona. Then I walked a long way in falling snow and darkness from the Sulmona station to the hotel I had called ahead to, far out of the way but the only one with a room I could get for the night. It felt like I walked in that frigid night for an hour before getting there. Alone in my room, I fell asleep, warm and grateful.

Upon awaking I stepped out into a sunny morning that inspired me with hope as I gazed at a sublime, snow-covered mountain filling half the azure sky before me and smiling down benevolently. The darkness of the night had obscured it when I had arrived at the hotel, so this was a pleasant surprise as I am rather fond of mountains. I would learn later that this mighty titan was the Majella, and on opposite sides of it lay the villages of my grandparents. My hope renewed, I made the long walk back to the Sulmona station, my next goal to travel to Guardiagrele, the hometown of my grandfather Giovanni Ranieri. I had to wait some time before the first train, so I explored the ancient city, finely decorated with aqueducts and romanesque medieval architecture. Then, strolling into Piazza XX Settembre, a bronze statue atop a high marble pedestal caught my eye and I approached to investigate. It was Ovid's statue! the Roman poet whose verses I had first read in *Lingua Latina*. Ovid's was the first Latin poetry I had ever read in the original thanks to that book. Some months previous when I read those words of his I took them down in a commonplace notebook that I kept with me:

> *Non ego nobilium sedeo studiosus equorum;*
> *cui tamen ipsa faves vincat ut ille precor.*
> *Ut loquerer tecum veni tecumque sederem,*
> *ne tibi non notus quem facis esset amor.*
> *Tu cursus spectas, ego te — spectemus uterque*
> *quod juvat, atque oculos pascat uterque suos!*

In this scene from the *Amores (III.2)*, Ovid is with his girlfriend Corinna at the Circus Maximus watching a horse race. These lines may be translated as follows:

> Though I am sitting here, it's not in the least
> because I am interested in the racing; all the
> same, I want your favorite to win. What I've
> come here for is to talk with you, to sit near you,
> and to tell you how tremendously I love you.
> So you are looking at the races, I am looking at
> you. Let us both enjoy the sight that pleases,
> both drink our fill of delight.

I retrieved my notebook from my pack and looked for the poem. But why was Ovid's statue here in Sulmona, just a stone's throw from my grandparents' hometowns? The inscription below the statue informed me: because Ovid was born in Sulmona! Thus Ovid and I were kinsmen, I realized with a grin, both from Abruzzo. Quite moved, I read aloud those six lines of Latin before the idol to their author. But more effort to commemorate the meeting felt warranted. Those lines came in the final chapter of *Lingua Latina*, and the pleasure of understanding them arrived after three months of intense effort to master the language. It had been the sweetest reward. And only five months later I was standing in the man's birthplace and in his statue's shadow. I studied his brow, heavy and lined with the sorrows of his exile, his eyes alive with romance. He was even carrying a notebook like my own, to pen his latest poetry no doubt. Turning my gaze downward to the open commonplace, I used my recall technique to memorize the poem in a few minutes. I put my notebook away, and recited the lines once more while admiring the bronze figure sculpted by Ettore Ferrari. Then I patted his sandaled foot with my hand and made for the station. To this day I have never forgotten those verses.

PRACTICE SECTION

1. Commit to memory the Preamble to the United States Constitution, transcribed here:

We the People of the United States, in Order to form a more perfect Union, establish Justice, insure domestic Tranquility, provide for the common Defense, promote the general Welfare, and secure the Blessings of Liberty to ourselves and our Posterity, do ordain and establish this Constitution for the United States of America.

2. Learn the poem *The Road Not Taken* by Robert Frost:

Two roads diverged in a yellow wood,
And sorry I could not travel both
And be one traveler, long I stood
And looked down one as far as I could
To where it bent in the undergrowth;

Then took the other, as just as fair,
And having perhaps the better claim,
Because it was grassy and wanted wear;
Though as for that the passing there
Had worn them really about the same,

And both that morning equally lay

In leaves no step had trodden black.

Oh, I kept the first for another day!

Yet knowing how way leads on to way,

I doubted if I should ever come back.

I shall be telling this with a sigh

Somewhere ages and ages hence:

Two roads diverged in a wood, and I—

I took the one less traveled by,

And that has made all the difference.

3. Learn Abraham Lincoln's Gettysburg Address:

Four score and seven years ago our
fathers brought forth on this continent, a new
nation, conceived in Liberty, and dedicated to
the proposition that all men are created equal.

Now we are engaged in a great civil war,
testing whether that nation, or any nation so
conceived and so dedicated, can long endure.
We are met on a great battle-field of that war.
We have come to dedicate a portion of that
field, as a final resting place for those who here
gave their lives that that nation might live. It is

altogether fitting and proper that we should do this.

But, in a larger sense, we can not dedicate — we can not consecrate — we can not hallow — this ground. The brave men, living and dead, who struggled here, have consecrated it, far above our poor power to add or detract. The world will little note, nor long remember what we say here, but it can never forget what they did here. It is for us the living, rather, to be dedicated here to the unfinished work which they who fought here have thus far so nobly advanced. It is rather for us to be here dedicated to the great task remaining before us — that from these honored dead we take increased devotion to that cause for which they gave the last full measure of devotion -- that we here highly resolve that these dead shall not have died in vain — that this nation, under God, shall have a new birth of freedom — and that government of the people, by the people, for the people, shall not perish from the earth.

CHAPTER 6

LEARNING GEOLOGY, TEACHING ITALIAN, & GETTING INTO PLAYS

M Y LAST DAYS IN ITALY DURING MY STUDY ABROAD program were in preparing for my final exams in Ancient Greek, Modern Greek, and Latin literature. All these were oral exams. Most notably I remember preparing for the Latin exam, which required reciting certain texts from Vergil's Georgics and Eclogues. So I memorized the texts, and then was able to read them with fluid understanding and subdued theatricality. I was proud to have received the Italian equivalent to a 100% on that exam. Miraculously, I received the same score on the other two exams, thanks entirely to my recall technique.

Upon my return to the States, and having achieved my life's dream of being in Italy, I realized it was time to pursue a new dream, and that was to change my major to geology. I had come to miss science which I had loved from an early age thanks to Bill Nye and the Discovery Channel, and I had loved being outside as a kid, so the fit seemed quite natural. I am grateful that my alma mater Lehigh University in Bethlehem, PA, was accommodating. Once I switched majors, I was very pleased that the geology department actually had a professor who was Italian-American and spoke the language fluently, and moreover due to his connexions with geologists at the University of Bologna there were Italian graduate students working in the department! How is *that* for serendipity? I felt at home.

But there were challenges ahead. I had a lot of catch-up work to do, now a junior and not having had taken any of the prerequisite science courses. I also needed basic mineralogy and petrology classes. Ranieri Reverse Recall came to the rescue! I applied my method to the periodic table in chemistry, to kinematics formulas in physics, and to the memorizing of mineral compositions. Perhaps most useful of all was my Latin and Greek, for the vast majority of scientific terms, particularly in geology, are derived from the Classical languages. And since those terms are eponymous, I could decipher most of them by their name alone without the need for a definition. You can imagine I was extremely grateful for my previous efforts.

While earning my bachelor's of science, I had a new job in the evenings as an Italian teacher. For whatever confounding reasons, Italian language courses were cancelled at my university while I was abroad. So the study abroad department, which still was sending dozens of students to Florence annually, needed something to help their participants pick up some of the language before shipping them out. As I had gone further in my study of Italian through that program than any other at my school, I was offered the job of teaching night classes there. I loved it immediately, and I am indebted to my patient fellow college students who came to my lessons and helped me to become a teacher. It would remain my part-time job for the rest of college.

And it was here that I really saw the rapid results of Ranieri Reverse Recall in others. I used it to help them pronounce long or difficult words, and to learn verb conjugations. By then I was sure I was on to something.

I also had the opportunity to perform roles in a few college plays. My recall technique was instrumental in my learning the lines quickly. During those years I also decided to learn French, and was able to internalize the verbs and other inflected forms hastily thanks to their similarity to Latin and Italian, and thanks most of all to using my memorization technique combined with the Dowling method described above. I cannot envision what my life would have been like without Ranieri Reverse Recall.

PRACTICE SECTION

1. Memorize the names of the periodic table elements in order.

2. Learn part or all of this soliloquy from *Hamlet* by William Shakespeare:

> To be, or not to be, that is the question:
> Whether 'tis nobler in the mind to suffer
> The slings and arrows of outrageous fortune,
> Or to take arms against a sea of troubles
> And by opposing end them. To die—to sleep,
> No more; and by a sleep to say we end
> The heart-ache and the thousand natural shocks
> That flesh is heir to: 'tis a consummation
> Devoutly to be wish'd. To die, to sleep;
> To sleep, perchance to dream—ay, there's the rub:
> For in that sleep of death what dreams may come,
> When we have shuffled off this mortal coil,
> Must give us pause—there's the respect
> That makes calamity of so long life.

For who would bear the whips and scorns of time,

Th'oppressor's wrong, the proud man's contumely,

The pangs of dispriz'd love, the law's delay,

The insolence of office, and the spurns

That patient merit of th'unworthy takes,

When he himself might his quietus make

With a bare bodkin? Who would fardels bear,

To grunt and sweat under a weary life,

But that the dread of something after death,

The undiscover'd country, from whose bourn

No traveller returns, puzzles the will,

And makes us rather bear those ills we have

Than fly to others that we know not of?

Thus conscience does make cowards of us all,

And thus the native hue of resolution

Is sicklied o'er with the pale cast of thought,

And enterprises of great pitch and moment

With this regard their currents turn awry

And lose the name of action.

CHAPTER 7

SPANISH QUESTS
& FLIGHTS OF FANCY

W HEN I WAS OFFERED A JOB TEACHING LATIN AND
Spanish at a local middle school after I had
graduated from college in 2008, I knew I was well prepared
for the Latin, but underprepared for the Spanish. So, having
been offered the job just two weeks before the interview, I had
to learn Spanish to a more advanced level quickly. By then I
had Latin, Italian, and French to fall back on, so it was mainly
a matter of learning the Spanish verb conjugation paradigms,
and then how Spanish differed from the other three in terms
of vocabulary and other unique expressions. As you may
have guessed, this required plenty of Ranieri Reverse Recall to

make the Quixotic endeavor possible. I would be lying if I said I wasn't sweating bullets in the interview!

The job was mine. I was enthralled with the opportunity to teach and learn more about pedagogical techniques. And I would regularly use my recall method in my classes to help these sixth, seventh, and eighth graders retain long words, whole expressions, and learn verb conjugation paradigms. Thus then I knew people of all ages could take advantage of my invention.

That school year I also started flying lessons, and by August 2009 I had earned my private pilot's license. But making that happen with a full-time job was arduous, not least of all because of all the facts and terminology that pilots must learn. During the forty-five minute drive to the airport each weekend in Alexandria, NJ, and then back home again, I would recite aloud the facts I needed to know by heart. Another technique that accelerated my progress was making recordings of my voice dictating the various important things to know, and I would pause the audio periodically to memorize the ideas.

In planning my solo cross country flights, I planned backwards as well. I started from the end-point and built the plan in reverse order, up to my time of departure. I divided the flight into discrete segments separated by checkpoints. Then I rehearsed the whole flight from the last checkpoint to the end; then the second-to-last checkpoint all the way to the end; and so forth. When I actually performed the flight it felt very much as if I had already flown it, which made the experience much easier and quite relaxing.

PRACTICE SECTION

1. Depending on your level of ambition and desire to challenge yourself, learn one, two, or all three paragraphs of Winston Churchill's remarks at his alma mater the Harrow School in 1941:

> Never give in, never give in, never, never, never, never. In nothing, great or small, large or petty, never give in except to convictions of honor and good sense. Never yield to force. Never yield to the apparently overwhelming might of the enemy.

> We stood all alone a year ago, and to many countries it seemed that our account was closed; we were finished. All this tradition of ours, our songs, our school history, this part of the history of this country, were gone and finished and liquidated.

Very different is the mood today. Britain, other
nations thought, had drawn a sponge across her
slate. But instead our country stood in the gap.
There was no flinching and no thought of
giving in; and by what seemed almost a miracle
to those outside these islands, though we
ourselves never doubted it, we now find
ourselves in a position where I say that we can
be sure that we have only to persevere to
conquer.

2. Memorize part or all of *O Captain! my Captain!* by Walt
Whitman:

O Captain! my Captain! our fearful trip is done,
The ship has weather'd every rack, the prize we sought is won,
The port is near, the bells I hear, the people all exulting,
While follow eyes the steady keel, the vessel grim and daring;
But O heart! heart! heart!
O the bleeding drops of red,
Where on the deck my Captain lies,
Fallen cold and dead.

O Captain! my Captain! rise up and hear the bells;
Rise up—for you the flag is flung—for you the bugle trills,
For you bouquets and ribbon'd wreaths—for you the shores a-crowding,
For you they call, the swaying mass, their eager faces turning;
Here Captain! dear father!

This arm beneath your head!
It is some dream that on the deck,
You've fallen cold and dead.

My Captain does not answer, his lips are pale and still,
My father does not feel my arm, he has no pulse nor will,
The ship is anchor'd safe and sound, its voyage closed and done,
From fearful trip the victor ship comes in with object won;
Exult O shores, and ring O bells!
But I with mournful tread,
Walk the deck my Captain lies,
Fallen cold and dead.

CHAPTER 8

HIGH FLYING AIR FORCE

D ARKNESS OUTSIDE IN THE COOL, EARLY HOURS. CHILLED, but none dared shiver. My eyes caged forward in a thousand-yard stare. The streetlights glaring in my vision's periphery. Petrified with fear. Frozen in the position of attention, stiff uniform holding me upright. My equally foolish comrades by my side. All by choice.

Then: the face of the inspector. His harsh countenance, examining me up and down. Not impressed. He paused as he studied my eyes for the slightest deviation from looking straight ahead. Finding none, he inquired: "Cadet Ranieri, what is the fourth article of the Military Code of Conduct?"

Hesitation. Pounding pulse. Memory absent.

Angry face. "Let's hear it!"

Heartbeat. No words came.

In the latter half of 2009 occurred many such scenes. For graduate school I had made my way to San Diego State University. The rigors of earning a master's degree were notable, but the challenges to which I was subjected as a cadet in Air Force ROTC truly changed my outlook. The experiences were extremely edifying. Contrary to my previous stereotypical image of military training, the situations we were put into made me feel *more* human, not less. I found compassion and fraternity with young men and women I otherwise might never have associated with. For that alone I was deeply grateful.

Given that I had been an adult and was performing a full-time job the year prior to the scene described above made the epiphanies all the more humbling. Senior cadets more than a few years younger than I were giving me orders and teaching me how to be an officer. Yet I learned so much from it! Even terrifying events like forgetting the fourth article of the Code of Conduct while being inspected by an intimidating figure are almost as dear to me now as childhood memories. I laugh at myself upon recollecting them.

But at the time, I wasn't laughing. Nor was the inspector. I had to produce a paragraph verbatim, under stress and at the position of perfect military attention. The consequences were more PT (physical training), and I was exhausted already from hours of it under duress. The night before, however, I had memorized the paragraph in my backwards way. All I had to do was get the first words out… "If I become a prisoner of war…" I began, just in the nick of time to halt the inspector from demanding I pound the pavement, "…I will keep faith with my fellow prisoners. I will give no information or take part in any action which might be harmful to my comrades. If I am senior, I will take command. If not, I will obey the lawful orders of those appointed over me and will back them up in every way." Silence then. I only blinked and breathed. Satisfied, the hungry vulture moved on.

Here is how I had memorized the fourth article:

back them up in every way.

and will back them up in every way.

those appointed over me and will back them up in every way.

I will obey the lawful orders of those appointed over me and will back them up in every way.

If not, I will obey the lawful orders of those appointed over me and will back them up in every way.

I will take command. If not, I will obey the lawful orders of those appointed over me and will back them up in every way.

If I am senior, I will take command. If not, I will obey the lawful orders of those appointed over me and will back them up in every way.

which might be harmful to my comrades. If I am senior, I will take command. If not, I will obey the lawful orders of those appointed over me and will back them up in every way.

or take part in any action which might be harmful to my comrades. If I am senior, I will take command. If not, I will obey the lawful orders of those appointed over me and will back them up in every way.

I will give no information or take part in any action which might be harmful to my comrades. If I am senior, I will take command. If not, I will obey the lawful orders of those appointed over me and will back them up in every way.

I will keep faith with my fellow prisoners. I will give no information or take part in any action which might be harmful to my comrades. If I am senior, I will take command. If not, I will obey the lawful orders of those appointed over me and will back them up in every way.

If I become a prisoner of war, I will keep faith with my fellow prisoners. I will give no information or take part in any action which might be harmful to my comrades. If I am senior, I will take command. If not, I will obey the lawful orders of those appointed over me and will back them up in every way.

In recounting these stories, a certain training event comes to mind. Allow me to paint the image. Having already been exhausted by the usual 4 A.M. PT session, we formed up in the middle of some courtyard in an unpopulated part of campus (thankfully there were not many students out before sunrise), and were issued fake M16 rifles which are called rubber ducks, though they look and feel real. In a short practical class there in the dark under the street lamps we were given an abbreviated course in small unit infantry tactics, specifically how to move stealthily to engage the enemy. And then the simulation began.

In retrospect I can't believe our trainers got away with this, particularly considering California's aversion to guns, even fake ones. Luckily we were never spotted. I guess we were pretty stealthy.

One of us was made the squad leader, and he named a deputy from among us. Then the head trainer took our squad leader aside to give him the mission. The rest of us could not hear what he was told. Our squad leader joined us again and ordered us to move out, when suddenly a simulated explosion: "BOOM!" shouted a trainer in the face of the squad leader. "You're dead!"

The "deceased" squad leader, theoretically mute, then attempted to pass on the details of the mission to his deputy, which he had not done while he was "alive."

"Nope!" interrupted the head trainer. "You had your chance to tell your deputy about the mission before you left. It's too late now. Deputy, you're in charge."

"But what do we do? Where do we go?" cried the new leader.

The head trainer, with all the glower of a cold father dishing out tough love, replied, "I guess you'll just have to figure that out on your own. Hopefully you don't *all* die."

The resulting carnage would be infamous.

Comical in retrospect and painful at the time, this lesson made an impact on all of us, and its message encouraged me to begin writing this book. "Share information," the head trainer would harangue us later on that morning. "Don't keep information to yourself. It won't do anyone any good if you die."

So I taught my Ranieri Reverse Recall technique to the other cadets I was training with, and we were able to make the task of memorizing long passages of text much easier. As I inferred above, these are exceedingly pleasant memories for me. And my favorite of the passages we learned was a poem by John Gillespie Magee, Jr. This young American of only 18 years had volunteered to join the Royal Canadian Air Force in order to help defend England during the Battle of Britain, before the United States entered the war. At 19 he was posted to the UK in his Spitfire squadron, and strapped into that magnificent aircraft that took him as high as 33,000 feet for the first time in his life, he was inspired to write his sonnet *High Flight*:

Oh! I have slipped the surly bonds of earth,
And danced the skies on laughter-silvered wings;
Sunward I've climbed, and joined the tumbling mirth
Of sun-split clouds, — and done a hundred things
You have not dreamed of — Wheeled and soared and swung
High in the sunlit silence. Hov'ring there
I've chased the shouting wind along, and flung
My eager craft through footless halls of air...
Up, up the long, delirious, burning blue
I've topped the wind-swept heights with easy grace

Where never lark or even eagle flew —
And, while with silent lifting mind I've trod
The high untrespassed sanctity of space,
Put out my hand, and touched the face of God.

Pilot Officer Magee died in a training accident a few
months later. But his poetic soul has resonated with pilots and
admirers of airmen for generations. Having recently become a
private pilot in 2009 and aspiring to become a military aviator,
I found these verses to be profoundly evocative. If you find
them meaningful as well, join me in learning them by heart:

Put out my hand, and touched the face of God.

The high untrespassed sanctity of space,
Put out my hand, and touched the face of God.

And, while with silent lifting mind I've trod
The high untrespassed sanctity of space,
Put out my hand, and touched the face of God.

Where never lark or even eagle flew —
And, while with silent lifting mind I've trod
The high untrespassed sanctity of space,
Put out my hand, and touched the face of God.

I've topped the wind-swept heights with easy grace
Where never lark or even eagle flew —
And, while with silent lifting mind I've trod
The high untrespassed sanctity of space,
Put out my hand, and touched the face of God.

Up, up the long, delirious, burning blue
I've topped the wind-swept heights with easy grace
Where never lark or even eagle flew —
And, while with silent lifting mind I've trod
The high untrespassed sanctity of space,
Put out my hand, and touched the face of God.

My eager craft through footless halls of air...
Up, up the long, delirious, burning blue
I've topped the wind-swept heights with easy grace
Where never lark or even eagle flew —
And, while with silent lifting mind I've trod
The high untrespassed sanctity of space,
Put out my hand, and touched the face of God.

I've chased the shouting wind along, and flung
My eager craft through footless halls of air...
Up, up the long, delirious, burning blue
I've topped the wind-swept heights with easy grace
Where never lark or even eagle flew —

And, while with silent lifting mind I've trod
The high untrespassed sanctity of space,
Put out my hand, and touched the face of God.

High in the sunlit silence. Hov'ring there
I've chased the shouting wind along, and flung
My eager craft through footless halls of air...
Up, up the long, delirious, burning blue
I've topped the wind-swept heights with easy grace
Where never lark or even eagle flew —
And, while with silent lifting mind I've trod
The high untrespassed sanctity of space,
Put out my hand, and touched the face of God.

You have not dreamed of — Wheeled and soared and swung
High in the sunlit silence. Hov'ring there
I've chased the shouting wind along, and flung
My eager craft through footless halls of air...
Up, up the long, delirious, burning blue
I've topped the wind-swept heights with easy grace
Where never lark or even eagle flew —
And, while with silent lifting mind I've trod
The high untrespassed sanctity of space,
Put out my hand, and touched the face of God.

Of sun-split clouds, — and done a hundred things

You have not dreamed of — Wheeled and soared and swung
High in the sunlit silence. Hov'ring there
I've chased the shouting wind along, and flung
My eager craft through footless halls of air...
Up, up the long, delirious, burning blue
I've topped the wind-swept heights with easy grace
Where never lark or even eagle flew —
And, while with silent lifting mind I've trod
The high untrespassed sanctity of space,
Put out my hand, and touched the face of God.

Sunward I've climbed, and joined the tumbling mirth
Of sun-split clouds, — and done a hundred things
You have not dreamed of — Wheeled and soared and swung
High in the sunlit silence. Hov'ring there
I've chased the shouting wind along, and flung
My eager craft through footless halls of air...
Up, up the long, delirious, burning blue
I've topped the wind-swept heights with easy grace
Where never lark or even eagle flew —
And, while with silent lifting mind I've trod
The high untrespassed sanctity of space,
Put out my hand, and touched the face of God.

And danced the skies on laughter-silvered wings;
Sunward I've climbed, and joined the tumbling mirth

Of sun-split clouds, — and done a hundred things
You have not dreamed of — Wheeled and soared and swung
High in the sunlit silence. Hov'ring there
I've chased the shouting wind along, and flung
My eager craft through footless halls of air...
Up, up the long, delirious, burning blue
I've topped the wind-swept heights with easy grace
Where never lark or even eagle flew —
And, while with silent lifting mind I've trod
The high untrespassed sanctity of space,
Put out my hand, and touched the face of God.

Oh! I have slipped the surly bonds of earth,
And danced the skies on laughter-silvered wings;
Sunward I've climbed, and joined the tumbling mirth
Of sun-split clouds, — and done a hundred things
You have not dreamed of — Wheeled and soared and swung
High in the sunlit silence. Hov'ring there
I've chased the shouting wind along, and flung
My eager craft through footless halls of air...
Up, up the long, delirious, burning blue
I've topped the wind-swept heights with easy grace
Where never lark or even eagle flew —
And, while with silent lifting mind I've trod
The high untrespassed sanctity of space,
Put out my hand, and touched the face of God.

As this work has great resonance for me, I like to enjoy it from time to time, as people who appreciate literature may return to their libraries to pick up a good book or find a famous poem. But unlike them, we now do not have to return to the book. If you truly love a poem like I love this work, take a few minutes to learn those verses by rote. Then it will be with you always, ready to inspire you, to console you, to make you laugh or cry whenever you desire.

PRACTICE SECTION

1. Learn the Articles of the Military Code of Conduct:
    Article I: I am an American, fighting in the forces which guard my country and our way of life. I am prepared to give my life in their defense.
    Article II: I will never surrender of my own free will. If in command, I will never surrender the members of my command while they still have the means to resist.
    Article III: If I am captured I will continue to resist by all means available. I will make every effort to escape and aid others to escape. I will accept neither parole nor special favors from the enemy.
    Article IV: If I become a prisoner of war, I will keep faith with my fellow prisoners. I will give no information or

take part in any action which might be harmful to my comrades. If I am senior, I will take command. If not, I will obey the lawful orders of those appointed over me and will back them up in every way.

Article V: When questioned, should I become a prisoner of war, I am required to give name, rank, service number and date of birth. I will evade answering further questions to the utmost of my ability. I will make no oral or written statements disloyal to my country and its allies or harmful to their cause.

Article VI: I will never forget that I am an American, fighting for freedom, responsible for my actions, and dedicated to the principles which made my country free. I will trust in my God and in the United States of America.

2. Learn by heart another poem from my days as an Air Force cadet, *One More Roll*, by Captain Gerald L. Coffee, a Navy pilot shot down and imprisoned for seven years in North Vietnam in 1966. He composed this work while he was a prisoner of war:

> We toast our faithful comrades
> Now fallen from the sky
> And gently caught by God's own hand
> To be with him on high.

To dwell among the soaring clouds
They knew so well before
From dawn patrol and victory roll
At heaven's very door
And as we fly among them there
We're sure to hear their plea-
"Take care my friend; watch your six,
and do one more roll... just for me."

CHAPTER 9

―――――――

JAPAN

WHEN THE AIR FORCE SENT ME TO TOKYO, I KNEW I HAD a golden opportunity. Previously I had paid well for my study abroad program in Italy, so I knew how much of a gift it was to receive a salary to work in a foreign country. Naturally I took to learning the language as quickly as possible.

Once I had the right textbook (namely Tae Kim's Grammar Guide), the mission was to know by heart all the grammatical forms, much as I had done with Latin, French, and Spanish years earlier. It is amazing how much groundwork can be accomplished by learning grammar tables. My previous language experience combined with Ranieri Reverse Recall proved sufficient to become fluent in

Japanese in three months of living there. Its grammar is actually fairly simple, I discovered, if bizarre to Westerners. After a year I had organized my own Japanese language course into night classes for Americans living on the military base, a part-time job that I adored. It was enormous fun.

One of my favorite expressions to teach my students was お疲れ様です, *otsukaresamadesu*, "keep up the good work." I made a video for YouTube wherein one can see my use of Ranieri Reverse Recall in action. After explaining the individual parts of this term, I help the viewer to pronounce it through building backwards:

desu
(sounds like 'dess')

sama - desu

samadesu

kare - samadesu

karesamadesu

otsu
(sounds like "oats")

otsu - karesamadesu

otsukaresamadesu

This is a favorite phrase in Japanese but rarely taught to beginners. Japanese words aesthetically benefit from an abundance of vowel sounds, but that same overflowing of vocality makes it hard for Western ears to pick up new expressions easily. Although I was befuddled by the length of Japanese words at first like any English speaker, ultimately it was not a problem because I would always practice a long new word by sounding it out backwards. To this day I recommend the technique strongly to my students.

Helping my Japanese friends to pronounce English words was a regular task. English is much harder for the Japanese to learn than for English speakers to learn Japanese. This is for phonetic as well as grammatical reasons, but the difficulty of pronouncing the long strings of consonants inherent in our own tongue is a serious obstacle for our Eastern friends. Many common words from English are used in Japanese, but they scarcely resemble our versions. A well-known example is "McDonalds" which in Japanese is マクド ナルド, *makudonarudo,* which is the best they could do given their phonotactic limitations. It is easy for us to say, but coaching my Tokyo friends to gradually build the word backwards was instrumental to their success.

PRACTICE SECTION

1. Learn the Japanese word for "goodnight" : おやすみなさい *oyasuminasai.*

2. Pronounce the expression for "happy birthday" : おたんじょうびおめでとうございます *otanjoubi omedetou gozaimasu.*

3. The first time I wanted to arrange a dinner date with a Japanese young woman I liked, I thought I would impress her by calling ahead and making the reservation for us. Now, speaking fluently on the telephone in a foreign language is a task all of its own, and in Japan it is compounded by the vital importance of facial expressions and body language to establish context, which most languages can establish through words alone. So there is a lot of guesswork involved. But brave, or certainly brazen, I dove in, and memorized a few phrases to rattle off on the phone in order to ensure a smooth transaction, including "I would like to reserve a table by the window for two at 7 P.M." : 七時に二人の為の窓際のテーブルの予約をお願いします。 *Shichiji ni futari no tame no mado-giwa*

73

no teeburu no yoyaku wo onegai shimasu. Having worked to memorize phrases like these allowed them and their variants to become automatic in all my future dealings. If you're up for a demanding exercise, master this one as well!

CHAPTER 10

FLIGHT SCHOOL

IN 2015, I TRANSFERRED FROM ACTIVE DUTY AIR FORCE to the Army National Guard to become a helicopter pilot, and went straight to Army flight school that summer. My ability to commit things to memory has never been more intensely challenged! It felt just like being a cadet again, and those recollections of freezing outside in the darkness trying to remember lines came back to me. Except now the numbers and words to recall would either save my life or get me killed up there.

For example, take the definition of the emergency action term "Land as soon as possible" :

The term <u>LAND AS SOON AS POSSIBLE</u> is defined as landing at the nearest suitable landing area (e.g., open field) without delay. (The primary consideration is to ensure the survival of occupants.)

This, like many parts of the operator's manual, must be committed to memory and recited verbatim on the command of an instructor pilot. This is how I would start to learn this text:

the survival of occupants.)

to ensure the survival of occupants.)

(The primary consideration is to ensure the survival of occupants.)

without delay. (The primary consideration is to ensure the survival of occupants.)

(e.g., open field) without delay. (The primary consideration is to ensure the survival of occupants.)

nearest suitable landing area (e.g., open field) without delay. (The primary consideration is to ensure the survival of occupants.)

landing at the nearest suitable landing area (e.g., open field) without delay. (The primary consideration is to ensure the survival of occupants.)

The term <u>LAND AS SOON AS POSSIBLE</u> is defined as landing at the nearest suitable landing area (e.g., open field) without delay. (The primary consideration is to ensure the survival of occupants.)

I would divide the text into manageable chunks, logical pieces that helped me to understand the meaning while ingraining the precise words. Another technique I would employ would be to type the pieces out to help me memorize them, much as I had done with the *Lingua Latina* book ten years prior. Some prefer to write by hand for such a purpose, believing the manual process of penning ink onto paper to be more helpful for recall. Having grown up both typing and writing by hand from a young age (and being a user of the Dvorak keyboard layout, an ergonomic arrangement of the keys which comes with all computers), I find the manual process of typing equally helpful as a kinesthetic aid, and opine that the two-handed event of typing may in fact be *more* beneficial to memory by engaging both sides of the brain in the task. But as I am no neurologist I can only speak for my preference, and encourage the reader to employ whatever tactic works best.

Here is one of several dozen emergency procedures for the Black Hawk helicopter (the underlined steps must be known verbatim):

ENGINE FIRE IN FLIGHT

WARNING: Attempt to visually confirm fire before shutdown or discharging extinguishing agent.

1. <u>**Establish single engine airspeed.**</u>
2. <u>**ENG POWER CONT lever (affected engine) — OFF.**</u>
3. <u>**ENG EMER OFF handle — Pull.**</u>
4. <u>**FIRE EXTGH switch — MAIN/RESERVE as required.**</u>
5. <u>**LAND AS SOON AS POSSIBLE.**</u>

Note that the last step in this emergency procedure is to land as soon as possible, which we just studied above. That means, on demand, a pilot must be able to recite the above emergency steps, and then recall verbatim the paragraph for landing as soon as possible. Multiply the integration of pages and pages of emergency procedures with the complex knowledge required of the combat aircraft's myriad systems and you can see how taxing flight school can be, and how hard a professional pilot, military or otherwise, will work to maintain his proficiency. This is how I memorize it:

LAND AS SOON AS POSSIBLE.

MAIN/RESERVE as required.
LAND AS SOON AS POSSIBLE.

FIRE EXTGH switch — MAIN/RESERVE as required.
LAND AS SOON AS POSSIBLE.

Pull.
FIRE EXTGH switch — MAIN/RESERVE as required.
LAND AS SOON AS POSSIBLE.

ENG EMER OFF handle — Pull.
FIRE EXTGH switch — MAIN/RESERVE as required.
LAND AS SOON AS POSSIBLE.

OFF.
ENG EMER OFF handle — Pull.
FIRE EXTGH switch — MAIN/RESERVE as required.
LAND AS SOON AS POSSIBLE.

ENG POWER CONT lever (affected engine) — OFF.

ENG EMER OFF handle — Pull.

FIRE EXTGH switch — MAIN/RESERVE as required.

LAND AS SOON AS POSSIBLE.

Establish single engine airspeed.

ENG POWER CONT lever (affected engine) — OFF.

ENG EMER OFF handle — Pull.

FIRE EXTGH switch — MAIN/RESERVE as required.

LAND AS SOON AS POSSIBLE.

before shutdown or discharging extinguishing agent.

Establish single engine airspeed.

ENG POWER CONT lever (affected engine) — OFF.

ENG EMER OFF handle — Pull.

FIRE EXTGH switch — MAIN/RESERVE as required.

LAND AS SOON AS POSSIBLE.

WARNING: Attempt to visually confirm fire before

shutdown or discharging extinguishing agent.

Establish single engine airspeed.

ENG POWER CONT lever (affected engine) — OFF.

ENG EMER OFF handle — Pull.

FIRE EXTGH switch — MAIN/RESERVE as required.

LAND AS SOON AS POSSIBLE.

ENGINE FIRE IN FLIGHT

WARNING: Attempt to visually confirm fire before shutdown or discharging extinguishing agent.

Establish single engine airspeed.

ENG POWER CONT lever (affected engine) — OFF.

ENG EMER OFF handle — Pull.

FIRE EXTGH switch — MAIN/RESERVE as required.

LAND AS SOON AS POSSIBLE.

I find it helpful to memorize an off-beat enjambment like "Pull. FIRE EXTGH switch…" as one of the steps in my recall method because this helps my brain to connect the end of the item with the next item. It is much like learning the cues from other actors' lines for a play, prompting me to flow automatically to the phrase that will follow.

So then, as before, it is just a matter of rehearsal and being able to remember the first item; the lines that follow will flow more fluidly than the steps that precede. To drive the point home, let us examine the turbine gas temperature limits of the Apache helicopter's 701C engine:

949 °C: Maximum (>949 °C red)

904-949 °C: Single engine transient, 12 sec (yellow)

879-903 °C: Single engine contingency, 2.5 min (yellow)

852-878 °C: Maximum rated power, 10 min (yellow)

811-851 °C: Intermediate rated power, 30 min (yellow)

810 °C: Maximum continuous power

0-810 °C: Normal operation (green)

To further complicate matters, this list is read from the last item *upwards* to the top, imitating how the readout appears on the display. Thus we can apply Ranieri Reverse Recall in this way:

Maximum (>949 °C red)

949 °C: Maximum (>949 °C red)

Single engine transient, 12 sec (yellow)
949 °C: Maximum (>949 °C red)

904-949 °C: Single engine transient, 12 sec (yellow)
949 °C: Maximum (>949 °C red)

Single engine contingency, 2.5 min (yellow)
904-949 °C: Single engine transient, 12 sec (yellow)
949 °C: Maximum (>949 °C red)

879-903 °C: Single engine contingency, 2.5 min (yellow)
904-949 °C: Single engine transient, 12 sec (yellow)
949 °C: Maximum (>949 °C red)

Maximum rated power, 10 min (yellow)
879-903 °C: Single engine contingency, 2.5 min (yellow)
904-949 °C: Single engine transient, 12 sec (yellow)
949 °C: Maximum (>949 °C red)

852-878 °C: Maximum rated power, 10 min (yellow)
879-903 °C: Single engine contingency, 2.5 min (yellow)
904-949 °C: Single engine transient, 12 sec (yellow)
949 °C: Maximum (>949 °C red)

Intermediate rated power, 30 min (yellow)
852-878 °C: Maximum rated power, 10 min (yellow)
879-903 °C: Single engine contingency, 2.5 min (yellow)
904-949 °C: Single engine transient, 12 sec (yellow)
949 °C: Maximum (>949 °C red)

811-851 °C: Intermediate rated power, 30 min (yellow)
852-878 °C: Maximum rated power, 10 min (yellow)
879-903 °C: Single engine contingency, 2.5 min (yellow)
904-949 °C: Single engine transient, 12 sec (yellow)
949 °C: Maximum (>949 °C red)

Maximum continuous power
811-851 °C: Intermediate rated power, 30 min (yellow)
852-878 °C: Maximum rated power, 10 min (yellow)

879-903 °C: Single engine contingency, 2.5 min (yellow)

904-949 °C: Single engine transient, 12 sec (yellow)

949 °C: Maximum (>949 °C red)

810 °C: Maximum continuous power

811-851 °C: Intermediate rated power, 30 min (yellow)

852-878 °C: Maximum rated power, 10 min (yellow)

879-903 °C: Single engine contingency, 2.5 min (yellow)

904-949 °C: Single engine transient, 12 sec (yellow)

949 °C: Maximum (>949 °C red)

Normal operation (green)

810 °C: Maximum continuous power

811-851 °C: Intermediate rated power, 30 min (yellow)

852-878 °C: Maximum rated power, 10 min (yellow)

879-903 °C: Single engine contingency, 2.5 min (yellow)

904-949 °C: Single engine transient, 12 sec (yellow)

949 °C: Maximum (>949 °C red)

0-810 °C: Normal operation (green)

810 °C: Maximum continuous power

811-851 °C: Intermediate rated power, 30 min (yellow)

852-878 °C: Maximum rated power, 10 min (yellow)

879-903 °C: Single engine contingency, 2.5 min (yellow)

904-949 °C: Single engine transient, 12 sec (yellow)

949 °C: Maximum (>949 °C red)

If you actually took the time to memorize that just now, consider yourself an honorary pilot for the day.

It seems all that preparation years ago, standing at attention in the cold at zero-dark-thirty, was a discipline paying off here, and I took for granted how much easier it made the whole flight school experience for me. Don't get me wrong — remembering all this was still hard, very hard, and I made my share of mistakes that embarrassed me quite a bit. But that's all part of the experience of flight school. In study groups with my classmates I showed others how to do Ranieri Reverse Recall, and many of my friends found it useful and they started to employ it on their own which made me glad.

Interestingly, the basic idea of my technique is used already by assault pilots in planning a mission. The mission planner starts with the exact minute the troops need to get off the helicopter. He works backwards from the last checkpoint to that drop off including the landing formation of all the helicopters. The route there is planned to avoid enemy contact. And all this leads back to the beginning: the exact time the choppers should lift off in formation. I had experimented with this flight planning method when I was earning my private pilot license in 2009, and was pleasantly surprised to find that it was Army doctrine.

PRACTICE SECTION

How are your multiplication tables? Rusty, you say?
Why bother memorizing these math facts when my voice-
activated smart phone does the task for me, you ask? I answer
that you will be able to remember *more* things in life if you
exercise your mind in this way. The brain needs exercise like a
muscle. Moreover, if you do need to perform an arithmetic
calculation, your mind will be free to explore more
complicated approaches to the problem because your
unconscious mind will deliver the answer to you effortlessly.
Start with the last number in the column, and then build
backwards:

1	2	3	4	5	6	7	8	9	10	11	12
2	4	6	8	10	12	14	16	18	20	22	24
3	6	9	12	15	18	21	24	27	30	33	36
4	8	12	16	20	24	28	32	36	40	44	48
5	10	15	20	25	30	35	40	45	50	55	60
6	12	18	24	30	36	42	48	54	60	66	72
7	14	21	28	35	42	49	56	63	70	77	84
8	16	24	32	40	48	56	64	72	80	88	96
9	18	27	36	45	54	63	72	81	90	99	108
10	20	30	40	50	60	70	80	90	100	110	120
11	22	33	44	55	66	77	88	99	110	121	132
12	24	36	48	60	72	84	96	108	120	132	144

CHAPTER 11

LONG-TERM MEMORY

R ANIERI REVERSE RECALL IS AN EXCELLENT METHOD FOR approaching rote memorization. In order to create lasting recollection, however, there are other ideas I would recommend. Some techniques for attaining permanent recall were noted above, and these and more will be mentioned.

For Latin, I used Ranieri Reverse Recall to get a verb conjugation or noun declension pattern completely into my short-term memory. The next step was to write that paradigm down on paper without looking at the original text. So I would fill a whole page repeating it from rote. If I could then turn the paper over, and write it again without error and without peeking, I would know I had succeeded in memorizing it. If I made a mistake, I would repeat the process from the beginning until I could reproduce the paradigm. *Never* force yourself through a more complicated sequence to memorize without first fortifying the foundation.

From there begins the long-term memorization. Some say eighty times, while others say 200 times is the necessary count to repeat something so that it stays in long-term memory for the rest of one's life. Every person is different, I imagine, but this very high number seems to be adequate for nearly all individuals. In the case of the Latin paradigms, I rewrote them from short-term memory 200 times each. This was per the Dowling Method of brute memorization, and I still recall all of them today. This technique can be applied to any language, indeed, to any discipline that requires the rote recollection of information.

There is one element in this process which Dowling leaves out, but I found it to be essential in accelerating the process. Before starting your repetitions for long-term memory, make sure you already have committed the sequence to short-term memory using Ranieri Reverse Recall. If you drag yourself through a thousand scrawled words without knowing exactly what should come next, if you have to refer constantly to the template, you will take much longer to really learn it. I have only my experience to guide this opinion. Nevertheless, if you take my advice and apply my recall technique *first*, you will comfortably and rapidly have the thing in short-term memory. From there, begin your repetitions. This may take minutes, hours, or days. Each successful repetition will extend the shelf-life of the memory in another indeterminable amount of time, which may be different for each person and variable even for a certain person given conditions of alertness. Eventually, somewhere just prior to 200 times, the memory becomes indelible.

I accept the hypothesis that all memories may decay with time, something akin to a neurological sort of half-life. However, it seems possible to so completely ingrain a thing that its neurological half-life is much longer than the normal human lifespan. Thus it becomes a memory for the rest of one's time on earth.

While a person may have a preference for learning style, it is important to appeal to all one's learning abilities. A kinesthetic type learner should exercise reading retention, and a visual learner should employ audio. And to stimulate auditory memory I have recorded my own voice reciting basic military knowledge for in my cadet days, Russian grammar paradigms, helicopter manual chapters, and others. I find that hearing one's own voice makes the process especially memorable due to the familiarity of the sound.

For learning the numbers of a foreign language, I mentioned that a long-term memory technique is to name any digits you see throughout the day in the target language. This is vital because numbers and math in another tongue are exceptionally hard to internalize. I also recommend this to my students to telling time; once you have learned to tell time in a foreign language, you had better declare the time out loud on every clock and watch your eyes pass, every single day for a week or more.

To stimulate kinesthetic memory, I recommend counting aloud in the target language any repetitions of a normal activity, such as push-ups or other exercises. When you are tired and in the middle of a strenuous activity, you will be amazed how hard it becomes to remember a thing, and even harder then to do the physical exercise because of the mind sucking up your energy in that moment. This difficulty, however, is precisely why you *must* challenge yourself in this way. After doing ten unusually difficult crunches while counting in, say, Spanish, you will find the next time and the times after that inordinately easy to count *and* to perform the exercise. The counting becomes easier because your mind associates it with the movements of the body. And the crunches become easier because your mind is meditative and distracted from the physical exertion. Consider this before turning on the TV while at the gym. Self-improvement can be made very efficient. In order to ingrain into long-term memory both the Airman's Creed and Soldier's Creed, I would do plank abdominal exercises after using Ranieri Reverse Recall to capture the lines in short-term memory.

A final recommendation I would like to give is for the free online software program called Anki (from the Japanese word for "memory") which uses the Leitner Method, a system for using flashcards to retain information in long-term memory. The Leitner Method was designed for paper flashcards, and has the student place flashcards whose answers he knows into a pile which he will not touch for several days. Unknown cards are reviewed each day until they are learned. Once they are learned, they may go to the pile to be studied three days later. When it comes time to review a card from the three-day pile, it moves to the seven-day pile. And so on and so forth, the cards that are forgotten or need memorizing are reviewed each day, and the ones that are known are not seen for days, weeks, or months. In this manner information can be etched permanently into long-term memory.

The Anki software and website do all this card shuffling for you digitally, removing the labor and maximizing the efficiency of the process. Another free website that leverages the Leitner Method is Remembering the Kanji used for the Chinese characters used in the Japanese writing system. I have used this website with great success to teach myself the kanji of Japanese and I recommend it for my students as well.

CONCLUSION

A S MOTIVATION TO START YOU ON ADOPTING MY RECALL technique in your daily life, I would like to leave you with a final comment from Oscar Wilde's *The Importance of Being Earnest*: "Memory, my dear Cecily, is the diary we all carry about with us." Even though the author intended this line to be humorous, it resonates with me nonetheless. Whatever your spiritual or philosophical tenets with respect to human existence and what may lie beyond, you may agree with me that who we think we are is founded on what we remember of our own past. A tinge of paradoxical circularity infuses these pages on memory, as they are mostly about recollections from my own life — a life whose principal events were influenced profoundly by the process of making memories. I would not be the same person without them. Since Mnemosyne, the Greek deity of memory, is the mother of all the muses, it seems the Greeks are advising us to give respect to our power of recollection, for she is the source of all our inspiration.

ABOUT THE AUTHOR

*Luke Amadeus Ranieri is an Aviation Officer and pilot in the
Arizona Army National Guard. He has ratings in the TH-67 Creek,
OH-58A/C Kiowa, and UH-60A/L Black Hawk helicopters. Ranieri
also gives private lessons in Japanese, Italian, Latin, and others in
his free time. Read more about his projects at
www.LukeRanieri.com.*

Printed in Great Britain
by Amazon